Miracle
IN THE
Making

The incredible

story of the

making of

Left Behind II:

Tribulation Force

RAY COMFORT

Bridge-Logos *Publishers*

Gainesville, Florida 32614 USA

Miracle in the Making: The Incredible Story of the Making of *Left Behind II: Tribulation Force*

Published by:
Bridge-Logos Publishers
P.O. Box 141630
Gainesville, FL 32614, USA
www.bridgelogos.com

Edited by Lynn Copeland

Cover, page design, and production by Genesis Group

Cover photos by Ken Woroner

Printed in the United States of America

ISBN 0-88270-931-3

Unless otherwise indicated, Scripture quotations are from the *New King James* version, ©1979, 1980, 1982 by Thomas Nelson Inc., Publishers, Nashville, Tennessee.

Photos from *Left Behind II: Tribulation Force* courtesy of Cloud Ten Pictures; used by permission.

My sincere thanks to
Cloud Ten Pictures
&

Namesake Entertainment,
who have done so much to
further the gospel in these closing
hours of time. Eternity will reveal
the results of their labors.

Contents

Foreword

Ray Comfort is a little man on a *big* mission. I don't know whether to call him a lunatic, a man on fire for the Lord, or just a normal, biblical Christian. Traveling with Ray is like trying to keep up with a five-year-old boy in a toy store—every time I turn around, he's gone! Just when I'm sure he's exhausted every possible opportunity to speak with people about eternal life, he's found another one. A police officer, a desk clerk, a passenger, a waiter. In airports, hotels, and restaurants; on airplanes and elevators; even in public restrooms—anywhere! We've come close to missing flights, being arrested, and getting punched out, all because Ray won't quit.

The wonderful thing about watching him in action is seeing the wake of smiles he leaves behind. What a thrill to see long lines of people waiting to board their planes reading "$1 million bill" tracts, laughing at the "World's Funniest One-Liners," and even going out of their way to ask him for more for their friends. In all my years of learning about God and His wonderful ways, I have never met anyone from whom I've learned as much, or with whom I've been so grateful to spend time, as this little lunatic from New Zealand named Ray Comfort.

KIRK CAMERON

Introduction

Filmmaking is a collaborative process. No one person can make a great movie. From the writers to the director to the actors and the hundreds of people behind the camera, everyone plays a role that greatly affects the outcome of the final movie.

The key ingredient is passion. Nowhere is this truer than in making a Christian film. I remember the day Kirk called me a few weeks before filming began. He said he had some ideas for the script. He was very polite and said he understood that it was not the role of actors to be writers, but he had some thoughts on how the gospel content could be further strengthened.

I was thrilled, because I had just had a meeting with the writers (which included my brother, Paul) about doing the exact same thing, and Kirk's ideas were terrific. Of course, I later learned the whole story of Kirk and Ray that you are about to read in this book. It will thrill your heart as it has mine. This is a great story of faith, commitment, and dedication to the kingdom. And it is a story I saw played out in real life.

But, Kirk's contribution was not just in writing. Kirk and Chelsea's passion for their faith filled the whole set. And when it came time for their major scenes in the movie, they hit it out of the park.

I could not be happier to be associated with them, and we look forward to getting together and working with Kirk and Ray on *Left Behind III* as well!

PETER LALONDE
CEO
Cloud Ten Pictures

CHAPTER ONE

Left Behind at the Airport

It was May 2001. I had just watched the first of the *Left Behind* movie productions. The series of *Left Behind* books had been a runaway bestseller and the movie had followed in its steps, selling millions of copies. The movie was well-made, and I enjoyed seeing Kirk Cameron play the lead part. He had been in a number of major motion pictures and was so popular that during the seven-year production of the TV sitcom "Growing Pains" he received 10,000 fan letters each week. The movie had many wonderful references to God, the Bible, prayer, etc., and some salvation scenes showing the power of God's grace. But I would have loved to have seen the gospel even more fully presented. I know now that the producers had the same sentiment. In an evangelistic enterprise such as the making of a major motion picture, the challenge is ensuring that it is truly a movie and not just a thinly disguised sermon, since that would no doubt turn off the audience. However, I wondered how much further the boundary could be pushed. Could the gospel have been even more clearly presented without undue offense?

Some months before seeing the movie, my son-in-law EZ had spoken with the son of Jerry Jenkins, the co-author of the *Left Behind* series. The son told EZ that they were involved in a major *Left Behind* movie production starring Kirk Cameron. EZ introduced me and I took the opportunity to give him an audiotape of "Hell's Best Kept Secret"[1] to pass on to his dad. This is a teaching that expounds the importance of using the Ten Commandments to show us that we need God's forgiveness.

Just prior to that incident, my associate, Mark Spence, and I had attended the Christian Bookseller's Association (CBA) convention to promote my latest publication. We had seen Tim LaHaye, the other series co-author, standing at the Atlanta airport and decided to introduce ourselves. We soon learned that the famous author had been left behind after missing his flight.

I was surprised to find that he traveled alone and said, "I always travel with an associate. All it takes nowadays is for some woman to rub against you, accuse you of touching her inappropriately, and your ministry can been slurred." He smiled and said, "Son, when you are my age, no woman rubs up against you." We laughed, and I took the opportunity to get his address so I could send him a copy of "Hell's Best Kept Secret."

We didn't give him one personally because our supply of tapes had run out. Mark had given dozens to authors and other well-known Christian celebrities at the convention. I was proud of Mark's boldness. Instead of standing in line with hundreds of others, he would go to the front and say something like, "Excuse me. This is a tape you have just got to listen to," and then leave.

In a sense, the approach was easy for Mark because he so believed in the teaching. He had listened to the one-hour audiotape hundreds of times. He understood the importance of it and longed for others to see its great truths. He had even been able to get one into the hands of Kirk Cameron, who was at the CBA promoting *Left Behind: The Movie*. In Mark's usual bold fashion, he walked to the front of the line and said, "Excuse me, Kirk. You just have to listen to this teaching." Kirk was friendly, and graciously took the tape.

> We soon learned that the famous author had been left behind after missing his flight.

Celebrity Call

I get many phone calls, but a special sense of excitement gripped me with this one. I had been talking with one of the phone operators in our ministry when I heard my son Daniel say, "I recognized your voice." He then turned to me and said, "It's Kirk Cameron, from 'Growing Pains.'" I quickly walked to my office, picked up the phone, and heard a distinctive voice say, "Hi, Ray. I'm Kirk Cameron. You may know me as Mike Seaver from the 'Growing Pains' television series."

He then went on to tell me that he had listened to "Hell's Best Kept Secret." While in his car on his way to a church to speak, he had slipped the tape into the player. What he heard was so radically different from what he was about to preach that it threw him for a loop. He had no choice but to share the message he had prepared, and ask God to forgive him. Then he listened to the tape again. And again.

Kirk was very enthusiastic during our thirty-minute conversation, and asked if I would be available to have lunch some time.

After the call, I went to see what he had ordered. He had requested our "Excellence in Evangelism" 18-video series. This showed me that he was serious, so I picked up a copy of my book *Revival's Golden Key*, signed it, and placed the publication on top of the order.

The next day, my cell phone rang. It was Kirk. He had just watched the first video and said that he was devastated. He repeated that he wanted to meet with me for lunch, because he had so many questions about the teaching.

It was such an encouragement to know that a celebrity was genuine in his faith. Over the years many Hollywood stars have professed to be sincere, but time has revealed that their Christianity was just another acting job.

I'll Be Back

It was Monday around noon. I was a little nervous as I waited for a celebrity visitation. I don't think that I would have been more excited if the President had been coming for lunch. Through the years in Santa Monica, I had rubbed shoulders with a few stars. Sort of. I had had a brief conversation with Arnold Schwarzenegger.[2] Very brief. When I asked him if he would like a tract, he gave a very resolute "No!" and walked off. James Cameron, director of the movie *Titanic*, asked for one of our "Titanic" gospel tracts, which didn't surprise me because the tract goes down well. Ricky Schroeder ("Silver Spoons" and "NYPD Blue") intently listened to me preach for twenty minutes. I had two encounters with Cathy Lee Crosby, and Dennis Weaver once listened to me speak for nearly an hour (he didn't have any choice, as he was sitting in the front row of a church at which I was the guest speaker).

When my wife, Sue, told me that Kirk was in the parking lot, I went outside and greeted him as he got out of his car. We then walked inside together and I introduced him to the staff. A few minutes later, Rachel (my daughter), Mark, and I were heading off to hobnob with a Hollywood bigwig. How cool.

I have often felt the pressure not to be my usual

self when having lunch with pastors who were wanting me to speak at their churches. It's the pastor's chance to check me out before trusting me with his pulpit. Something in me would say, *Don't give out gospel tracts in the restaurant; be discreet. You will embarrass the pastor,* but I had learned to ignore it. I decided to ignore the thought on this occasion also.

As we entered the restaurant, I held up my wallet and showed my "ID" to the greeters. It is a computer-altered photo of me with my forehead stretched to about 14 inches. It looks ridiculous. It's the ultimate ice-breaker, and almost always gets laughs. It was once so appreciated by stressed airport staff that it was directly responsible for Mark and I being upgraded to business class.

Back in the restaurant, the staff packed around, partly because of the laughter at my photo and no doubt because they recognized Kirk Cameron. I took advantage of the situation and handed out gospel tracts to each person. When we sat at the table, I did some sleight-of-hand for the waiter and gave him one of our tracts, which he seemed to appreciate.

For the next three hours we sat in the restaurant and talked. During that time Kirk was asked if he would pose for photos with the staff, something he graciously did. He had many questions about what he had learned through the teaching. Fortunately, they were questions I had been asked before, and my answers seemed to satisfy him. Both Rachel and Mark had a good grip on the teaching and were also able to give valuable input to the conversation. As we left the restaurant, I visited the tables close to us and gave the occupants tracts.

After we got back to the ministry, it seemed that Kirk didn't want to leave. He stayed for another two hours, and even helped us load the UPS truck. He laughed at my humor, including the dumb photos I had placed on the walls of our building. This man had a gift of discerning quality humor.

When he left I felt a sense of sadness. Still, it was a memory we would all cherish.

Rocked Out of My Chair
The next day I received the following e-mail:

> Ray,
> For weeks, I had been looking forward to meeting with you, hoping to find a man of God. Instead I found a lunatic. Just kidding.
>
> I was so fired up after leaving your place! Your teachings on the Law and grace have made more sense to me than anyone else's, and I am so thankful for what God is doing…I believe I was robbed of the deep pain of seeing the depth of my sinfulness, of experiencing the exceeding joy and gratitude that comes from the cross, because I was convinced of God's love before I was convinced of my sin. I didn't see the big problem, but by faith believed I was a sinner (many worse than me, but nevertheless

a sinner), and repented of my "general sinful, selfish attitude." I had never opened up the Ten Commandments and looked deep into the well of my sinful heart. I never imagined that God was actually angry with me at a certain point because of my sin. Because of "grace," I kind of skipped over that part and was just thankful that He loved me and had promised me eternal life.

While I think I was saved thirteen years ago, I was rocked out of my chair last night, on my knees confessing the *specific* sins that have plagued my heart that were never uncovered before. I think my knowledge of the "new covenant" and "under grace, not Law" kept me from ever examining my heart by the light of the Ten Commandments. The new weight of my sin is causing more pain in me...wounding my ego, and showing me how much more Jesus had to pay to set me free. Oh, the wonderful cross!!!!

Over the next few months it became common to hear one of the staff buzz me and say, "It's Kirk." In fact it became quite normal to hear from him every day, and each call was as exciting as the first. We both decided that God had drawn us together and knit our hearts for a reason.

CHAPTER TWO

The Ultimate Statistic

I n was October 1971. Tears rolled from my eyes as I looked at my wife of just over one year. Sue was sound asleep, but I was wide awake. It seemed to me that most of humanity was in a spiritual deep sleep. They seemed to be living in a dream world, knowing that they had an appointment with death, but not waking up to it. I was very awake that night, face to face with life's harshest reality. That reality was the cold fact that my beloved wife could be torn from me by death at any moment. I couldn't understand why we were part of the ultimate statistic: ten out of ten die.

No one seemed to talk about the subject. Think of it—everyone you love, everything you hold dear will be torn from your hands by death. Each person is going to be swallowed by this great monster that no one spoke about. Science could put a man on the moon, but seemed to be ignoring the fact that we are aging and heading for death. Why didn't someone say,

"Hey, guys, we're all going to die. Let's look into what causes this big problem, and fix it"?

Those in the medical profession were just as bad. They seemed more worried about the common cold than the common grave. They strained at a gnat and swallowed a camel. A big, ugly camel. Life didn't make any sense because death made it futile.

Six months later I was on a surfing trip about one hundred miles from my home. It was there that a young surfing buddy helped me understand the biblical explanation of why we die. Even though I recited the Lord's Prayer each night, I never thought that God had much to do with life or death. My concept of the Creator was very shallow.

Pastor, Are You Alone?

While he was driving in Colorado Springs, a pastor was talking on his cell phone with his lawyer. The lawyer thought he heard a woman's voice in the background and asked the pastor if there was someone else in the car with him. The pastor replied that he was alone and continued the conversation. A few minutes later the lawyer distinctly heard a woman speaking in the background and again asked the pastor if someone was in the car with him. He again denied that anyone was with him. It seemed to the lawyer that the pastor was obviously lying, so he said, "I am going to get off the phone. It is in appropriate for me to be speaking with you."

Both were actually telling the truth. The lawyer

had heard a woman's voice speaking, and yet the pastor was alone in the car. The missing information is that the pastor's vehicle was connected to a global positioning satellite and the female voice that could be heard was audio, giving him directions. The pastor was so used to the sound of the voice in the background that he hardly noticed it as he spoke on the phone.

Perhaps you have heard voices in the past about the Christian faith that have shaped a particular impression of the Church. To you it lacks integrity and is full of hypocrites. You feel that it would be inappropriate for you to have anything to do with it. However, you are missing some important information. Here it is: There are no hypocrites in the Church. Hypocrites are *pretenders*, masquerading as genuine Christians. God sees the pretenders and He sees the genuine, and warns that they will be sorted out on Judgment Day. So make sure you are with the right group.

That night on the surfing trip I was given a lot of missing information. First, I discovered that each of us will die because we have sinned against a holy God. We have violated an eternal law—"The soul who sins shall die" (Ezekiel 18:4). I didn't see myself as being a particularly bad person, until I was confronted with one verse from the Bible: "You have heard that it was said to those of old, 'You shall not commit adultery.' But I say to you that whoever looks at a woman to lust for her has already committed adultery with her in his heart" (Matthew 5:27,28). I remember reading the first portion of the verse and saying, "Well, I haven't committed adultery, so if there is a heaven, I will probably make it." The rest of the verse dashed my hope of heaven into a thousand pieces. It was on April 25, 1972, that I discovered that God considers lust to be adultery and hatred to be murder. It was the greatest revelation of my life because it showed me that I needed God's forgiveness.

He Did Believe

One of the most thought-provoking incidents in the *Left Behind* movie was the fact that a pastor named Bruce Barnes was left behind. It seems strange that that happened. He did believe in God. He no doubt had "invited Jesus into his heart." He never missed a Sunday service. He read his Bible. He prayed. He preached. He even led others in prayers of salvation. He baptized believers. The man was a pastor! He seemed to be a model Christian, *yet he was left behind*. Why?

Jesus gives us the answer in Matthew 7:21–23. He warned that *many* would consider themselves Christians and yet not be saved. Jesus said, "Not everyone who says to Me, 'Lord, Lord,' shall enter the kingdom of heaven...Many will say to Me in that day, 'Lord, Lord, have we not prophesied in Your name, cast out demons in Your name, and done many wonders in Your name?' And then I will declare to them, 'I never knew you; depart from Me, you who practice lawlessness.'" Wow. Look at how committed people can be and still not make it to heaven:

- They called Jesus "Lord."
- They prophesied in His name.
- They cast out demons.
- They did many "wonders" in His name.

These people are more spiritual than most of us, and yet they will be rejected by the One they call "Lord."

Have you ever wondered if you will be one of those who will be rejected by Jesus in that day? How can you make sure that you're not? There is a way to know.

The key is in verse 23. Jesus said to them, "Depart from Me, you who practice *lawlessness*." That is a reference to something we rarely hear about these days. He is speaking of the Moral Law—the Ten Commandments. So if you want to make sure of your salvation, look seriously at the Ten Commandments and see for yourself how you will do on the Day of Judgment. For instance, the First Commandment says, "You shall have no other gods before Me." Is God first in your life? Have you always loved Him with all of your heart, mind, soul, and strength? Jesus said that your love for family, friends, and even your own life should be like hatred compared to your love and devotion to God. Kirk says something that I can certainly identify with. He said that before he became a Christian, his dirty socks were more important to him than God. How about you? Have you kept this Commandment?

What about the Second? "You shall not make for yourself an idol." Have you made a god to suit yourself? Have you ever created in your mind a god that you're more comfortable with, and believed something like, "God is a god of love and mercy who would never judge anyone or send anyone to hell"? What about "You shall not steal"? Have you ever stolen anything? (The value of the item is irrelevant.) Have you always been honest when paying taxes? How about "You shall not lie"? Have you ever told a fib, a white lie, a half-truth, or an exaggeration of the truth? You may not think that deceitfulness is a wicked sin, but God does. The Bible warns that all liars will have their part in the Lake of Fire (Revelation 21:8).

The Tenth Commandment says, "You shall not covet." Have you ever desired something that belonged to someone else? Then according to God's Word, you will not enter the kingdom of heaven.

How did you do? Will you be innocent or guilty on Judgment Day? No doubt you are like me and the rest of humanity, and you will be guilty. Do you think you'll go to heaven or hell? If you believe you'll go to heaven, why is that? Perhaps you are thinking that God is "good" and that He will therefore overlook your sins. Try that in a court of law. Imagine you have committed rape and murder. The judge says, "You are guilty. Do you have anything to say before I pass sentence?" and you say, "Judge, I believe that you are a good man, and therefore you will just let me go." The judge would probably say, "I *am* a good man, and it's because of my goodness that I will see to it that you are punished!" The truth is that if God gives you justice, you're not headed for heaven, but for hell. The very thing that you are hoping will save you on the Day of Judgment is the very thing that will condemn you. If God is "good," He must by nature punish murderers, rapists, thieves, liars, fornicators, adulterers, etc. Be sure of it, He will punish sin wherever it is found.

Take the time to do what the Bible says: "Examine yourself to see whether you are in the faith" (2 Corinthians 13:5). Many won't do this until the Day of Judgment, when the Commandments seek them out. In the meantime, they tell fibs and white lies, take things that belong to others, harbor bitterness in their hearts, covet the things of others, and have a wandering eye when it comes to the opposite sex. They don't see sin as being very sinful. However, God sees them as lying, thieving, greedy, hateful, adulterers at heart. That's why it is so important for us to see ourselves in truth, under the light of God's Law. Otherwise, we make the fatal mistake of thinking that God's standards are the same as ours, and that we have nothing to be concerned about. That is the ultimate deception.

Is this true of you? If so, consider this—despite your belief in God and your thought that you are a good person, if you died at this very moment, you would spend forever in hell because you have violated His Law. That is a terrifying thought. The Bible says that God's wrath abides on you. You are "an enemy of God in your mind" (Colossians 1:21). Scripture calls you a "child of wrath" (Ephesians 2:3).

Make Me

So what should you do? Simply give up your will; surrender to God. You must come to Him like the prodigal son, saying, "I have sinned against heaven. Make me like one of your hired servants." Confess your sins to God and repent (turn from your sins). Recognize that you broke God's Law and Jesus paid your fine—"God demonstrates His own love toward us, in that while we were still sinners, Christ died for us" (Romans 5:8). Look at Jesus suffering for you and realize that God's wrath came down upon the innocent Lamb of God so that you could go free. Do you understand that? Like Kirk, you will only appreciate the depth of God's love and forgiveness when you understand how deeply you have sinned against Him. If your understanding is shallow, ask God to show you your sin as it really is, and then ask Him to show you the cross in all its horror.

Jesus then rose from the dead and defeated death for all who obey Him. If, as I did, you realize you need God's forgiveness, pray something like this from your heart (use your own words): "Dear God, please forgive me for sinning against You. I confess and turn from my sins. Thank You that Jesus died on the cross for me. Today I place my trust in Him as the one and only Lord of my life. Please take away my selfishness and change my heart. Help me to reach out to those who are still in their sins. I pray in Jesus' name. Amen."[3] You can trust in God completely. He will never let you down.

Better Than Surfing

When I returned from that surfing trip, I was more than ecstatic. I had found out why we die, but more than that, I had found the answer to death. The moment I repented and placed my trust in Jesus, death lost its sting and I was given the gift of everlasting life.

As a new convert I told my buddies that I had found something that was better than surfing. They couldn't believe that there could be any such thing, but with my continual hounding, a number decided to experiment

> I had found out why we die, but more than that, I had found the answer to death.

and "prayed the sinner's prayer." Not because they realized they had sinned against God, but because they wanted to see if what I was saying was true. Within a very short time, almost all fell away from the faith, much to my dismay. I never fully understood why this happened until August 1982.

As the years went by, an itinerant ministry began to open to me, giving me access to church growth records. I was horrified to find that up to 90 percent of those who were making commitments to Christ were falling away from the faith.

One Friday afternoon I was sitting in my office reading a portion of a sermon by Charles Spurgeon. I was fascinated to find that the "Prince of Preachers" used God's Law (the Commandments) to cause his hearers to tremble. This is what I read that began a radical change in my life:

> There is a war between you and God's Law. The Ten Commandments are against you. The First comes forward and says, "Let him be cursed, for he denies Me. He has another god beside Me. His god is his belly and he yields his homage to his lust." All the Ten Commandments, like ten great cannons, are pointed at you today. For you have broken all of God's statutes and lived in daily neglect of His Commandments.
>
> Soul, you will find it a hard thing to go at war with the Law. When the Law came in peace, Sinai was altogether on a smoke and even Moses said, "I exceedingly fear and quake!" What will you do when the Law of God comes in terror; when the trumpet of the archangel shall tear you from your grave; when the eyes of God shall burn their way into your guilty soul; when the great books shall be opened

and all your shame and sin shall be punished . . . Can you stand against an angry Law in that day?

A few days later I was reading Galatians 3:24. However, instead of reading it as "The Law was our schoolmaster to bring us to Christ," I subconsciously read it as "The Law was a schoolmaster to bring *Israel* to Christ." The question suddenly struck me: "Is it legitimate to use the Law as a schoolmaster to bring sinners to Christ, just as it brought Israel to Christ?" So I closed my Bible, and began to search for a sinner on whom I could experiment.

When I found a gentleman who was open to the gospel, I took him through the Ten Commandments first, and then I shared the cross. He stood to his feet and said, "I've never heard anyone put that so clearly in all my life." It was like a light went on in both of our heads. He understood the gospel, and I began to understand the great principle that the Law was a schoolmaster that brings the knowledge of sin, convincing a sinner of his need for the Savior.

I immediately began to search the literature of men like John Wesley, Spurgeon, Whitefield, Luther, and others whom God had used down through the ages. I found they warned that if the Law wasn't used to prepare the way for the gospel, those who made decisions for Christ would almost certainly be false in their profession and would fall away.

At that time, Kirk was about to burst on the scene

with a smash hit sitcom. It would be another twenty years before our paths would cross, and we would work together on something that had the potential to affect the eternal destiny of millions.

CHAPTER THREE

Who's Tom Cruise?

Kirk mentioned that he and his wife, Chelsea, were considering doing another *Left Behind* movie, but there were problems with the first script they were sent. (Chelsea played flight attendant Hattie Durham.) The next day he called to say, "They've sent me another script. It is really good—I mean *really* good. I will e-mail this one to you. Let me know what you think."

I later learned that Cloud Ten Pictures, the Christian film studio producing the movie, made a deal with their production partner that allowed them to replace the original script with a more evangelistic one. What I had in my hands was the first draft of this completely transformed script.

I read the entire script in two hours. It *was* good. The story line held my attention, and as I read it I marked where I thought it could use additional gospel input. I went over it with Mark, then called Kirk. As I did so, I could hardly believe what we were doing. Only a year earlier I was watching the first *Left Behind* movie and imagining how the gospel could be further incorporated. Now I not only had in hand the script of perhaps the most anticipated prophecy movie ever, but I was suggesting revisions.

Although I didn't know it at the time, we were doing something that was not only unorthodox, but was an attempt at the impossible. The scriptwriters write the script. That's their job. Stars are paid big bucks to star in the movie; that's their job. No matter how big the name, they are rarely given permission to rewrite major portions of the script.

Nevertheless, we spent hours on the phone rewriting certain scenes, and acting them out to see if they sounded right. As I listened to Kirk give his thoughts, I was amazed at his maturity and understanding of the Scriptures. He wasn't just some Hollywood poster-boy who had simply added Jesus to his life, but a godly man and a gifted Bible teacher.

The next day Kirk called to inform me that he and Chelsea were seriously thinking of turning down their parts in the movie. He said that there were other difficulties beside the needed script changes. Filming was scheduled to start in two weeks, but contracts hadn't yet been signed. He wasn't even sure who the other stars would be. If he played opposite bad actors, it could damage his reputation. He seemed to have made up his mind, and tried to lessen any disappointment on my part by saying that he would send the producers the suggested script changes.

Such a Time as This

The following day I sent Kirk an e-mail:

> Kirk,
>
> It's early Sunday morning. I have been lying awake since 4:00 a.m. horrified at the thought of you not doing the movie. We've got a good solid friendship, so I feel at liberty to share my heart.
>
> Let's pull back and see what an opportunity is being given to you. When someone takes a tract from me, I am thrilled. Here is a possibility that a human may read the Word of God, and may sometime in the future come to a place of true repentance and find *everlasting life!* When I pour my heart out (preaching open-air) at Santa Monica and become subject to hatred, insults, and filthy language (like you wouldn't believe), in the back of my mind I am thinking that perhaps, among the hearers, there is someone who is listening and may find everlasting life. My great confidence is that I am doing what I have been commanded to, and that God's Word cannot return void.
>
> Through this movie you have an unprecedented opportunity to preach this incredible gospel (the whole counsel of God) to millions. Billy Graham may have reached one or two million in a year, but you can reach ten, perhaps twenty, million or more through one movie. If I were you, I would apply Paul's atti-

tude to this situation. Here it is:

"If I preach the gospel, I have nothing to boast of, for necessity is laid upon me; yes, woe is me if I do not preach the gospel! For if I do this willingly, I have a reward; but if against my will, I have been entrusted with a stewardship. What is my reward then? That when I preach the gospel, I may present the gospel of Christ without charge, that I may not abuse my authority in the gospel. For though I am free from all men, I have made myself a servant to all, that I might win the more;...I have become all things to all men, that I might by all means save some" (1 Corinthians 9:16–22).

Kirk, if I were you, I wouldn't look at this as an actor, but as a preacher. As an actor, you should be concerned about your reputation... but as a preacher of the gospel you can make yourself of no reputation.

Name one other human in history who has had the opportunity you are being offered. Perhaps you were born for such a time as this...

With all that said, whatever you decide is your business, and I will respect that. This is because our friendship comes a close second to the cause of the gospel. I can't tell you what a joy it is to be your friend. I thank God for bringing you into my life. Ray

He sent me an immediate reply. It simply said, "Praying hard." Although I thought it may jeopardize a very valuable friendship, I sent another e-mail:

> Kirk,
>
> A group of firefighters arrive at a building that is on fire. Dozens of people trapped on the sixth floor are screaming for help. Terrified onlookers sigh with relief when the firefighters arrive, but become frustrated that they aren't getting out of their vehicle. They find that the head firefighter is calling headquarters to see if he should attempt to rescue the people.
>
> There are some things a firefighter doesn't need to call headquarters about, and there are some things we need not even ask God about, because of the clear mandate He has given us. We have been told to "Go into all the world and preach the gospel to every creature," and to "Preach the Word! Be ready in season and out of season." When Jesus looked upon the multitude, there is no record that He sought the Father in prayer to see if He should feed them. There is no record that Peter prayed about whether he should preach to the unsaved on the Day of Pentecost. God knows that if He offered me what He has offered you, the only prayer I would pray is, "Thank you, Lord. What an opportunity; what an honor! For to me, to live is Christ" (the Living Bible says, "For to me, living means opportunities for Christ").
>
> You have told me that if you could just wait

for a door to open in the movie industry, instead of preaching to thousands (as you do now), you could preach to millions. It's here, Kirk. This is your opportunity. Perhaps it came quicker than you thought... it just didn't come in the fancy Hollywood wrapper.

Spurgeon said something like, "If God has called you to be a missionary, don't shrink down to be a king." If God has called you to be a preacher, don't shrink down to be Hollywood's greatest star. Stars fade so quickly. Despite reruns, this generation doesn't even know who Jimmy Stewart and Marlon Brando are. If the Lord tarries, in fifty years time they won't even know who Tom Cruise is, or his movies will be so low-tech they will be a joke.

How long do we have? Look at what's happening in Israel. These are the last moments of time. Seize the moment, Kirk. The script is excellent, and you have the opportunity to help lock in the gospel presentation. What more could you want? Ray

The next day Kirk called and said that he had received the second e-mail. He then laughed in a now familiar way, and sincerely thanked me for being forthright with him. He had decided to do the movie.

The next step was to talk with Peter and Paul Lalonde, who run Cloud Ten Pictures, and see if they'd be open to letting us work with them on the script—something that is just not done in the film industry.

CHAPTER FOUR

Why the Changes?

To illustrate why we felt the changes to the script were necessary, I am going to quote directly from the book that so spoke to Kirk, *Revival's Golden Key*. (This may seem a little out of place, but please stay with it because it has a very important point.)

Two men are seated in a plane. The first is given a parachute and told to put it on, as it would improve his flight. He's a little skeptical at first, since he can't see how wearing a parachute in a plane could possibly improve his flight.

After some time, he decides to experiment and see if the claims are true. As he puts it on, he notices the weight of it upon his shoulders and he finds he has difficulty in sitting upright. However, he consoles himself with the fact that he was told the parachute would improve his flight. So he decides to give it a little time.

As he waits, he notices that some of the other passengers are laughing at him because he's wearing a parachute in a plane. He begins to feel somewhat humiliated. As they continue to laugh and point at him, he can stand it no longer. He sinks in his seat, unstraps the parachute, and throws it to the floor. Disillusionment and bitterness fill his heart, because as far as he was concerned he was told an outright lie.

The second man is given a parachute, *but listen to what he is told.* He's told to put it on because at any moment he'll be jumping 25,000 feet out of the plane. He gratefully puts the parachute on. He doesn't notice the weight of it upon his shoulders, nor that he can't sit upright. His mind is consumed with the thought of what would happen to him if he jumped without the parachute.

The Motive and the Result

Let's now analyze the *motive* and the *result* of each passenger's experience. The first man's motive for putting on the parachute was solely to improve his flight. The result of his experience was that he was humiliated by the passengers, disillusioned, and somewhat embittered against those who gave him the parachute. As far as he's concerned, it will be a long time before anyone gets one of those things on his back again.

The second man put on the parachute solely to escape the jump to come. And because of his knowledge of what would happen to him if he jumped without it, he has a deep-rooted joy and peace in his heart knowing that he's saved from sure death. This knowledge gives him the ability to withstand the mockery of the other passengers. His attitude toward those who gave him the parachute is one of heartfelt gratitude.

Listen to what the modern gospel says: "Put on the Lord Jesus Christ. He'll give you love, joy, peace, fulfillment, and lasting happiness." In other words, Jesus will improve your flight. The sinner responds, and in an experimental fashion puts on the Savior to see if the claims are true. And what does he get? The promised temptation, tribulation, and persecution—the other passengers mock him. So what does he do? He takes off the Lord Jesus Christ; he's offended for the Word's sake; he's disillusioned and somewhat embittered; and quite rightly so. He was promised peace, joy, love, and fulfillment, and all he got were trials and humiliation. His bitterness is directed toward those who gave him the so-called "good news." His latter end becomes worse than the first—he's another inoculated and bitter "backslider."

Instead of preaching that Jesus improves the flight, we should be warning the passengers that they have to jump out of a plane. That it's appointed for man to die once, and after this the judgment. When a sinner understands the horrific consequences of breaking the Law of God, he will flee to the Savior solely to escape the wrath that's to come. If we are true and faithful witnesses, that's what we will be preaching: that there is wrath to come—that "God commands all men everywhere to repent, *because* He has appointed a day on which He will judge the world in righteousness" (Acts 17:30,31). The issue isn't one of happiness, but one of righteousness. The fact that the Bible doesn't mention the word "happiness" even *once*, yet mentions "righteousness" 289 times, should make the issue clear.

It doesn't matter how happy a sinner is, or how much he is enjoying the pleasures of sin for a season; without the righteousness of Christ, he will perish on the day of wrath. The Bible says, "Riches do not profit in the day of wrath, but righteousness delivers from death" (Proverbs 11:4). Peace and joy are legitimate *fruits* of salvation, but it's not legitimate to use these fruits as a drawing card *for* salvation. If we do so, the sinner will respond with an impure motive, lacking repentance.

Can you remember why the *second* passenger had joy and peace in his heart? It was because he knew that the parachute was going to save him from sure death. In the same way, as believers, we have joy and peace in believing because we know that the righteousness of Christ is going to deliver us from the wrath that is to come.

With that thought in mind, let's take a close look at an incident aboard the plane. We have a brand new flight attendant. It's her first day, and she's carrying a tray of boiling hot coffee. She wants to leave an impression on the passengers and she certainly does! As she's walking down the aisle, she trips over someone's foot and slops the hot coffee all over the lap of our second passenger. What's his reaction as that boiling liquid hits his tender flesh? Does he say, "Man, that hurt!"? Yes, he does. But then does he rip the parachute from his shoulders, throw it to the floor, and say, "That stupid parachute!"? No; why should he? He didn't put the parachute on for a better flight. He put it on to save him from the jump to come. If anything, the hot coffee incident causes him to cling tighter to the parachute and even look forward to the jump.

If we have put on the Lord Jesus Christ for the right motive—to flee from the wrath to come—then when tribulation strikes, when the flight gets bumpy, we won't get angry at God, and we won't lose our joy and peace. Why should we? We didn't come to Christ for a better lifestyle, but to flee from the wrath to come.

If anything, tribulation drives the true believer closer to the Savior. Sadly, we have multitudes of professing Christians who lose their joy and peace when the flight gets bumpy. Why? Because they are the product of a man-centered gospel. They came lacking repentance, without which we cannot be saved.

Tell Them About the Jump

How then do you convince a person that he needs the Savior? The same way you would convince someone that he needed to put on a parachute. You would simply tell him about the jump. You would reason with him about the foolishness of jumping 25,000 feet without a parachute. He must understand that there are terrible consequences when the law of gravity is violated. You would then let his natural reasoning do the rest.

When we reason with people using the Law of God (the Ten Commandments), it has the power to convince them of their danger. It shows them that they need a Savior. This was the key to the success of all the great preachers God has used down through the centuries, and this is what was missing both in the script and in the modern gospel.

Kirk and I wondered if Cloud Ten would be willing to incorporate this into their revised, already good script. After all, it was their money on the line. Although they were committed to the gospel, using the Law in evangelism is a new concept to many. We held our breath as Kirk approached them with our suggested additions and ideas. With all that was going on, I wondered how he would sleep that night.

CHAPTER FIVE

This Is Impossible

H ey, Ray. It's Kirk. I'm calling from Toronto. I've just spent forty-five minutes with one of the producers explaining the use of the Law in evangelism, *and he loves it!* I went through every illustration I know and he has seen its importance. This is wonderful!"

Kirk was very excited. I was too, because he had told me that outside of his initial conversion experience, he hadn't seen God do much in his life in the area of the supernatural. Now it seemed that he was beginning to see something miraculous take place.

I had seen God do many wonderful things in my thirty years as a Christian. One experience in particular helped me to know that nothing is impossible when it comes to God.

I regularly surf atheist web sites on the Internet. It was during one of these "surfing" days that I came up on the dry shores of the American Atheists, Inc. web site. I decided to ask them if they would allow me to speak at one of their conventions. After all, they were undoubtedly convinced that no one could prove the existence of God, and that if I were allowed to speak I would simply say that we must have "faith" to believe in God. That was an argument they could shoot down in flames, and therefore they might (it was a long shot), on that basis, allow me to speak.

I carefully formulated an e-mail asking if they would consider me as a guest speaker at their national convention. I explained that I had spoken extensively on the subject of atheism at Yale and other prestigious learning institutions. I had written a booklet called "The Atheist Test" that had sold over a million copies, as well as a book titled *God Doesn't Believe in Atheists: Proof That the Atheist Doesn't Exist.*[4]

They graciously declined my offer, which I took as a compliment, but I was disappointed. I had hoped that God would somehow do a miracle and open the door. On reflection, I was actually asking for the impossible. Imagine—an atheistic organization having a preacher as a guest speaker! How naïve.

Who's the Chicken?

Some time later I found myself crossing swords with Ron Barrier (the spokesperson for American Atheists, Inc.) via e-mail. At one point he asked if I would have the courage to face him in a debate at their national convention in Orlando, Florida. I told him that I would be delighted, and said that I would even pay my own airfare from Los Angeles to Florida.

He then read *God Doesn't Believe in Atheists* and quickly withdrew the offer. Shortly after that incident, a number of other atheists began writing to me, and when one called me a "chicken," I told him that it was Ron Barrier who deserved that title because he had "chickened" out of a debate. They didn't believe me, so I found his finger-lickin' good e-mail and forwarded it to them. They roasted him to a point where he admitted to it, renewed the offer, and then sweetened the pot by flying me at their expense from Los Angeles to Florida to debate at their 2001 national convention.

What I had hoped for was impossible—but with God *nothing* shall be impossible.

My video production manager, Ron Meade, went with me. They put us in a classy hotel and gave us a fruit basket with a welcome card. It was a wonderful experience. The debate was broadcast live on their web site, and they gave us permission to videotape it.[5]

Ron Barrier and I cosigned my book together for their library, and we even hugged after the debate. It was like a dream. What I had hoped for was ridiculous, bizarre, and ludicrous. It was impossible—but with God *nothing* shall be impossible.

One-Way Ticket Home
It was because of this, and other experiences, that I

felt we could believe that God could do anything. Kirk called to tell me that he discovered the two other producers lived a couple of hours away. He decided to rent a car and visit them because production was due to start in two days. If he didn't talk to them immediately, it would be too late to make any changes.

About two hours later Kirk was on the other end of the line again, but this time his voice was different. He said, "I rented a car and was about to leave when I found out that the producers aren't even home. Now I have been given the latest script, Ray, and there are big problems with it. It's not Cloud Ten's fault—we may just be out of time. What we were attempting to do was impossible anyway. I don't think we can get this done. I am considering getting a one-way ticket home."

We spent the next twenty minutes talking and came to the conclusion that there was no miracle without a lion's den. There is no resurrection without a body. There was no opening of the Red Sea without Pharaoh at the heels of Israel. Obviously there is no movie without a good script, but we decided to drop any "buts" and "what ifs," and trust God for a miracle. We were in for a surprise.

CHAPTER SIX

This Is a Miracle!

The next day Kirk asked me to send him quality quotations from great preachers of the past, commending the use of the Law in evangelism, as he was going to try to pull a meeting together. This is what I sent him:

> Kirk, here are the quotes:
>
> John Newton (wrote "Amazing Grace"): "Ignorance of the nature and design of the Law is at the bottom of most religious mistakes."
>
> Charles Spurgeon (the Prince of Preachers): "I do not believe that any man can preach the gospel who does not preach the Law... Lower the Law and you dim the light by which man perceives his guilt; this is a very serious loss to the sinner rather than a gain; for it lessens the likelihood of his conviction and conversion. I say you have deprived the gospel of its ablest auxiliary [most powerful weapon] when you have set aside the Law. You have taken away

45

from it the schoolmaster that is to bring men to Christ... They will never accept grace till they tremble before a just and holy Law. Therefore the Law serves a most necessary purpose, and it must not be removed from its place."

Jonathan Edwards (who preached the famous "Sinners in the Hands of an Angry God"): "The only way we can know whether we are sinning is by knowing His Moral Law."

George Whitefield: "First, then, before you can speak peace to your hearts, you must be made to see, made to feel, made to weep over, made to bewail, your actual transgressions against the Law of God."

John Wesley: "It is the ordinary method of the Spirit of God to convict sinners by the Law. It is this which, being set home on the conscience, generally breaks the rocks in pieces. It is more especially this part of the Word of God which is quick and powerful, full of life and energy and sharper than any two-edged sword."

Martin Luther: "The first duty of the gospel preacher is to declare God's Law and show the nature of sin."

C. S. Lewis: "When we merely say that we are bad, the 'wrath' of God seems a barbarous doctrine; as soon as we perceive our bad-ness, it appears inevitable, a mere corollary from God's goodness..."

Charles Finney: "Evermore the Law must

prepare the way for the gospel. To overlook this in instructing souls is almost certain to result in false hope, the introduction of a false standard of Christian experience, and to fill the Church with false converts...Time will make this plain."

John Bunyan (author of *Pilgrim's Progress*): "The man who does not know the nature of the Law, cannot know the nature of sin."

Kirk responded with a phone call to thank me for the quotes. I was pleased to hear the usual optimism in his voice as he told me that he was about to meet with the director and producers. He said, "Pray that God does a miracle. Pray hard."

Over the next four hours, I prayed. I prayed hard, like you would pray for a loved one who was in serious surgery.

Blow by Blow

Four hours later the phone rang. It was Kirk. I told him that I had said to Sue that either he was having a good, long meeting with the producers, or he was lying on the floor, discouraged and dejected, and it took him four hours to crawl to the phone.

He then held the phone away from his mouth and hollered, "Thank you, Lord!" He was ecstatic, and gave me a blow-by-blow account of what happened.

Before the meeting he asked me if I thought that he should show them a video. It was forty-five minutes of Kirk preaching major portions of "Hell's Best Kept Secret" at a huge church in San Diego. He delivered it with such God-given ability that the congregation gave him a standing ovation.

We decided that it was important to show the executives the video, as it would not only fully explain why the script additions were needed, but it would show them that Kirk was a sincere Christian and not just a Hollywood flake.

> By the end of the video, they were totally convinced that the changes were needed.

He spoke his piece, and then switched on the video. He paced around the room for the next forty-five minutes, thinking they were bored. But by the end of the video, they were totally convinced that the additional changes were needed, despite the impossible deadlines they were under—and remember that they had already changed the entire script just a few weeks before filming started. Kirk was thrilled to find that the producers had the same vision and were very open to the input. He kept saying, "This is a miracle! This is a miracle!" I had to agree. He was no longer in the lion's den.

Not only had the Lord been leading us in this direction, but Cloud Ten was fully committed to taking the movie in the same direction. This was certainly a completely different kind of film company!

On the set

Tribulation Force is the second movie from the *Left Behind* series (no. 3 on the *New York Times* all-time best-selling series list)

. . . and ACTION!

The director's view
(above)

Photo courtesy of Cloud Ten Pictures

Props

Preparing to shoot
a scene

Photo courtesy of Cloud Ten Pictures

"Chloe," one of the stars, and Kirk

Mark, Ray, and Kirk

Scaling the Wailing Wall on the set

Between "takes"

Ray sharing a tract with "Ray"

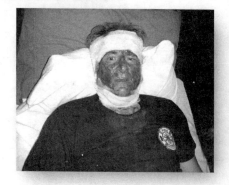

A burned firefighter from the movie

CHAPTER SEVEN

Well-oiled Machine

Things were moving so fast that it made our heads spin. It was late at night and Mark and I were sitting in the Los Angeles airport, waiting to take off on a red-eye flight to Toronto. Kirk had invited me to join him on the set. The last-minute ticket was very expensive, so I told Mark that he was welcome to join me if he could use his frequent flyer miles. However, the airline informed him that a 24-hour wait was required before mileage could be used. Mark thought for a moment, then said, "I am the associate of an author who has been working with Kirk Cameron on a movie script, and he wants us on the set." Suddenly the operator's demeanor changed. "Kirk Cameron! My husband used to be jealous because I had a crush on him. I'll see what I can do." Within minutes, Mark and I were booked to fly together to Toronto.

The next evening we joined Kirk on the *Left Behind* set. Nearly one hundred people milled back and forth, each with a specific set of duties. As Kirk's guests, we were treated like royalty. We were given food and drinks, and I was given earphones so I could hear the actors clearly, and my own "director's chair." It was amazing to see the precision with which everything worked. Like a well-oiled machine, the moment the director called "Cut!" dozens of people moved in with their particular expertise.

The set looked like the inside of a smoke-filled hospital room. It was actually a makeshift hospital in which lay the wounded and dying. The fake "smoke" was harmless, and gave atmosphere to the shoot.

In one bed lay a badly burned fireman. Amazingly, just a few days earlier Kirk and I had worked on this scene. The original script had him coming to God through the usual "sinner's prayer." I said that I wasn't a big fan of that method. My reasoning was that if a man has committed adultery and his wife is willing to take him back, should I have to give him a handwritten letter of apology to read to her? No. She isn't interested in his words. All she wants to know is if he is truly sorry for what he has done. That's why I think it is unwise to give a sinner (who is apologizing to God for sinning against Him) a "form" prayer. God isn't interested in his words, as much as He is interested in the sorrow of his heart.

So we proposed the following scene. The firefighter whispered, "I'm ready…" Chloe leaned forward to hear what the man was saying. He said, "I'm ready… for God…" She replied, "Then tell Him."

The burn victim's voice seemed to reveal that he

had more pain in his soul than in his body. He immediately whispered, "Oh, God . . . I'm sorry. I'm sorry for sinning against You. Thank You, Jesus, that You died for me. I give You . . . my . . . life." Then he breathed his last breath. It was a very moving scene.

The next day Mark and I went to a local park to preach open-air during the lunch hour, but there were only a few small groups of people rather than the crowds we had expected. When a group of high school kids arrived, I approached them with tracts, my stupid picture, and some sleight-of-hand. They loved it, took the tracts, and listened to every word I said. Mark recorded the encounter on video and that night we sat down with Kirk and viewed it together. He was free the next day, so we planned to go somewhere and preach open-air.

It rained . . . all day. Kirk wasn't due on the set until 8:00 that night, so we spent almost the entire time in our hotel room enjoying each other's company. Kirk even reenacted some of his favorite "Growing Pains" scenes for us. It was incredible. Our time of fellowship was interrupted only briefly while Kirk went through his lines with another cast member.

That night on the set I spoke with Jenny, who was in charge of wardrobe. She was in her early forties and was very friendly. She was intensely interested in the subject of God, so I shared a few thoughts between takes. When we parted that evening, I told her that the next day we could pick up where we left off. She seemed interested in doing that.

All That Garbage!

The following day I explained to Jenny about the small part I had played in revising the script. I explained that Kirk had read one of my books and seen the importance of incorporating certain principles into the movie. I told her that it was those very principles that made the Christian message make sense. She was deeply interested, so I took her through a few of the Ten Commandments. She had violated each of them, and saw that if she stood before God on the Day of Judgment, she would be in big trouble. When I stated that that was the reason Jesus died on the cross, she widened her eyes and replied, "That's something I never understood..."

As I explained that she had broken the Law and that Jesus had paid her fine, it was as though a light went on in her head. She now understood the Law, and therefore the gospel was no longer a foolish message to her.

I hoped that we could achieve the same result with the movie, so I was particularly interested in the scene they were about to shoot. This was a sequence that we had spent hours on.

> Chris burst out of the church. An hour or so earlier, Ray [and Buck, played by Kirk] had welcomed him into the meeting. Chris wasn't a Christian but he had reluctantly agreed to come. However, the pastor's mention of the Antichrist, sin, and judgment had made him

fume to a point of walking out of the meeting.

He angrily burst through the doors and out into the night. Ray followed hard on his heels and asked why he was so upset. Chris stopped in the semidarkness of the churchyard and spat out, "I can't sit there and listen to that garbage! "Save us from sin, Nicholae's the Antichrist"— come on. That's the problem with you people. You think everyone is 'bad.' Let me tell you something. There are a lot of good people in this world. Including me."

Suddenly a familiar voice asked, "According to whose standards—yours or God's?" It was Buck. He had followed Ray and Chris out of the church. Chris was taken aback with that question, and responded, "What?"

"You're a good person? Do you think you've kept the Ten Commandments?"

Chris said, "Yeah, pretty much. I'm not perfect, but I've never killed anybody."

"Have you ever lied?"

"Well, yeah. Who hasn't?"

"What does that make you?"

Chris retorted sarcastically, "Human."

"Come on, be honest. If you murder someone, it makes you a murderer. If you've lied, what does it make you?"

"Okay, a liar."

"Have you ever stolen anything? Even if it's something small?"

Chris winces a little as he says, "No. Well... yeah. Once."

"So what does that make you?"

Chris was beginning to get a little uncomfortable as he answered, "A thief."

"This is the one that got me. Jesus said that even if you look at a woman with lust in your heart, you've already committed adultery."

Chris laughed nervously. "Yep, guilty."

"Chris, by your own admission, you're a lying thief and an adulterer at heart, and that's only three of the Ten Commandments. If God judges you by those standards, will you be innocent or guilty?"

"I guess I'd be guilty."

"Chris, that's the point. When we stand before God, we're all guilty. If you don't get your heart right with God before that Day, you'll get the punishment you deserve. But that's not what God wants."

"What am I supposed to do? Get religious?"

Suddenly Ray butted in. "No, that's what we're trying to tell you. Jesus took the punishment for your sins upon Himself when He died on the cross. God did that so you wouldn't have to go to hell. That's how much God loves you. Eternal life is a gift. You don't have to do anything 'religious.'"

What happened to Chris after that? To find out ...you will have to see the movie.

CHAPTER EIGHT

The Celebrity Edge

As the three of us were having breakfast in the hotel in Toronto, Kirk mentioned, "I really want to use this platform God's given me to further the gospel." I told him that I am forced to use humor to break the ice with strangers so that I can share with them, but his celebrity gives him instant credibility even with strangers.

I then told him that I battle with fear every time I give anyone a tract. He was skeptical. Like most people who know of my "reputation," he mistakenly thought that I didn't have any fear. He admitted that he cringed with embarrassment the first time he went to a restaurant with me. He intentionally distanced himself from me over the next few weeks, but felt that God wanted him to also reach out to the lost, and even hand out a tract here and there. As time passed, he became convinced that gospel tracts were a legitimate means of evangelism. His reasoning was that if he was sitting in a restaurant and he really cared about the fate of unsaved people, he would try to reach them in some way. He surmised that perhaps he would grab a napkin and write, "Please take the time to read the Bible—consider your eternal salvation," fold it and pass it to a stranger as he left. That's basically what a tract is—a well-written gospel message on a classy napkin.

Over breakfast each of us shared our fears. We talked out how difficult it was to actually give a tract to someone due to the fear of being rejected. If someone took the tract, we would think, *Please don't open this until I leave!* We discussed our concerns that someone would take a tract and ask, "What is it?"

> I almost stepped
>
> on Kirk's heels as
>
> I whispered
>
> from behind,
>
> "Walk faster!"

Kirk looked at me and said, "Take for instance those four businessmen sitting at the next table. How would you approach them?"

As we ended our breakfast, he took four "Something to Think About"[6] tracts from his pocket and said, "Let me see how you do this." I picked up the tracts, walked a few paces to the other table and said, "Hello, gentlemen. Was the food okay?" They replied that it was great, and as they did so I said, "Here's something you may like to read when you have a moment." I placed the tracts on the table in front of them.

They were very congenial, and immediately looked at Kirk and asked him why his face was so familiar. I quickly introduced him and Mark. This was great. Kirk's celebrity was furthering our cause. The problem was, the men were flipping through the booklet as they talked. I felt like saying, "Put that down. Read it when we've gone. I want to wind up this conversation and make a quick getaway."

Suddenly, to the horror of the three of us, one of the men picked up a tract and asked, "What is this?" I quickly changed the subject by doing a sleight-of-hand routine, which greatly impressed them. Then, as we began to make our escape, the man asked again, "What is this?" This time there was no dodging the question. I reluctantly replied, "Oh, it's just a little gospel tract." The demeanor of all four men suddenly changed. The laughter fizzled, and they mumbled, "Oh...okay."

As we walked through the restaurant, Kirk led the way, feeling like the perpetrator of a bait-and-switch operation. I almost stepped on his heels as I whispered from behind, "Walk faster!" Then we started laughing, and the three of us broke into a run as we got out of the restaurant.

It was hard to believe, but almost everything we had talked about during breakfast happened in the minute or two that we spoke to the businessmen. Afterwards we had a frank discussion on why we wanted to get away. None of us were ashamed of the gospel, so why should we want to run?

Three answers come to mind. We were in a classy restaurant with other folks sitting at nearby tables, and if we had engaged in a conversation and there had been contention from the businessmen, we would have been (understandably) embarrassed. I was with two friends and if I had humiliated myself in some way, it would have been compounded by them witnessing it. And of course, our battle wasn't against flesh and blood. There were spiritual forces at work.

If you are a Christian, shouldn't you be using tracts to reach out to the unsaved? We can help you. Kirk and I have written tracts that are almost fun to give out (see www.WayOfTheMaster.com). Whatever you do, don't make the mistake of sitting in the fire engine while people are burning to death. Each of us has a moral obligation to rescue the lost, with the help of God.

Battle Strategies

Here are a few strategies to help in the battle if you fear rejection. Choose an environment in which it will be less likely for these fears to be realized. Start with someplace that, if worst comes to worst, will be more private than public. You may want to begin by yourself without the company of friends. Perhaps you could just leave a tract in an elevator or in a shopping cart, or hand out tracts as you leave a supermarket or restaurant parking lot. Choose a tract that you feel comfortable with. It may be one of ours that has plenty of "getaway time" ("101 of the World's

Best One-Liners"), or one that makes it abundantly clear to people what you are giving them ("Are You Good Enough to Go to Heaven?").

The bold approach may be easier than the undercover approach because at least there is no fear of being "discovered." Give a tract to a restaurant waiter or someone behind a counter as you are leaving a store. Be determined to handle rejection if it does come. If someone refuses to take the tract, try not to let that discourage you. After giving out hundreds of thousands, my greatest battle is with the devastation of having just one person say, "No, thank you!"— especially if I'm in the company of other people.

Mentally prepare your mind to be flooded with different fears. Learn to ignore them, or deal with them by quoting the Word of God—such as, "I can do all things through Christ who strengthens me" (Philippians 4:13). Prepare yourself to make a quick getaway from the battle scene if you wish. However, never forget the fact that you *are* in a battle. It is what the Bible calls the "good fight of faith," exhorting us to "fight." It is called "good" because there is no more worthy cause than the battle for the souls of men and women. So, make heaven rejoice.

Spiritual Growing Pains

The same day Mark and I arrived back in Los Angeles, Kirk called and was ecstatic. He had previously mentioned that he was tempted to share tracts with some film extras as they sat in the church waiting for a shoot, but he hadn't made the move. I suggested that if he gave a dead cockroach to each of the extras, they would take it home and put it in a glass case and say, "Kirk Cameron gave me this!"

The reason he was ecstatic when he called was that seventy-five extras on the set had each received a copy of "Something to Think About," and no one took offense. He added, "Ray, I was driving around Toronto thinking, *That would be a good place to do an open-air*. He laughed and asked, "What's happening to me?"

Breaking the Sound Barrier

As time passed, Kirk and I began to travel together for ministry. One weekend Kirk, his mom (who loves the Lord), and I went to Ohio for ministry. After the Saturday night meeting, we drove downtown to a festival to preach open-air. On the way there Kirk was tempted to speak, but felt the usual nerves we all feel. When he looked at me and said, "I've got a headache," I audibly prayed that it would

go away. After we found an area in the middle of a park, I began speaking and was able to attract a reasonable sized crowd, but after about twenty minutes a police officer told me to stop. When I asked if it was public domain (I knew it was), people in the crowd began calling out, "Let him speak!" The officer became so angry that I thought the veins in his neck were going to burst (and I was going to get arrested), so I asked him if there was someplace else I could preach. He kindly told me where to go.

We found another area about a hundred yards away and began speaking again. This time the atmosphere was much better. I spoke for about ten minutes then turned to Kirk and asked, "Do you want to give your testimony?" He had been thinking at that very moment, *This would be a good time to give my testimony*, and without hesitation jumped up on the box. I immediately went to the sidewalk, stopped groups of strangers, and asked them, "Have you heard of Kirk Cameron, from 'Growing Pains?'" When they said yes, I simply replied, "He's over there speaking"— and they rushed to the crowd like magnets. I was pumped. If I had had my act together, I would have organized a dozen Christians to do the same thing.

> I asked the officer if there was someplace else I could preach. He kindly told me where to go.

Kirk preached open-air three times that night. His mom even got up and spoke. This was such a big blessing. When we first met, Kirk wouldn't even hand out tracts because he was concerned about his image in Hollywood. If he was painted by the media as a fanatic, it could mean the end of any big movie roles. By open-air preaching, he wasn't just coming out of the closet—he was roaring out of the closet on a motorcycle. He told me later that when I prayed for his headache, it went away immediately. If you are wanting to preach open-air, be ready for some sort of hindering headache, but know that God is only too willing to remove it so that you can preach His gospel.

The Butterfly

Around that time Kirk asked me to join him at a meeting with executives from the movie's production company. We were picked up in a huge, white limousine. As four other men got in the vehicle, Kirk whispered to me who they were. One was the singer/songwriter whose songs include the well-known "Butterfly Kisses," and the others wore wigs that were just as big.

We were driven to a very classy restaurant and were seated at a table that was nothing short of "spiffing" (as the English say). One of the gentlemen began by telling Kirk and me, "I have just seen the second movie—the one where you two worked on the gospel presentation—and it is wonderful!" The man next to him agreed wholeheartedly (much to our joy).

I reached down into my bag and saw that I had a "butterfly" tract and decided that we could use it to scare the living daylights out of Mr. Butterfly Kisses (this tract has a printed butterfly that flies out of a card as it's opened). Kirk wrote on the envelope, "We appreciate you, etc.," and decided to give it to him just before dessert. Timing is everything.

A few minutes later our meals were served with a decorative butterfly on both of the plates. Mr. Butterfly...butterfly tract...butterfly meal...It was strange, so I whispered to Kirk that I thought God was going to take this lowly little ministry of ours and cause it to fly.[7]

At the conclusion of the meal we exchanged business cards, and I noticed that across the top of their cards were the words "Butterfly Group." That sent Kirk and I into a spin. (By the way, Mr. Butterfly jumped and then laughed. Ladies are better—they scream.)

With that encouragement from God, Kirk and I created a three-video series called "The Way of the Master," which contains "Hell's Best Kept Secret," "True and False Conversion," and "WDJD?" (What Did Jesus Do?). In the last video, we share the gospel with over a dozen people (including atheists) using the Law. We also established a web site called www.WayOfTheMaster.com, which has among its many features a very exciting training academy. In addition, we wrote a "Left Behind" tract with action pictures from the movie.

Cloud Ten Pictures was so excited about the soul-winning potential of the movie, and Kirk's passion for souls, that soon thereafter Kirk got a call from Peter Lalonde, the CEO of Cloud Ten. He offered to pay for and mail a copy of Kirk's message (in which he preaches the essence of "Hell's Best Kept Secret") to every youth group leader in the country who wants one! (Youth pastors can request a copy on the website www.C10youthpastors.com.)

Shortly after that, Kirk was giving out tracts wherever we went. He would pass them out when we entered a restaurant, and even go around the tables, and then hand out tracts when we left. I almost became used to people looking at him and with eyes like saucers, exclaiming, "Oh my gosh! Do you know who that was?" What a blessing.

CHAPTER NINE

Kissed or Cussed: The Power of Rejection

Kirk and I were with a couple of friends at a restaurant in Los Angeles. I moved outdoors from the bustle of the noise to take a call on my cell phone. As I was about to return, I passed a gospel tract to a woman who sat alone at a table. She looked at the tract, then to my surprise jumped up and kissed me on the cheek. I was delighted—not with the kiss, but with the woman's reaction to the tract.

A few weeks earlier we had been in an elevator in Florida, and I'd received a different response. A man to whom I had given a tract cussed at me, chewed me out, and spat what was left in little pieces onto the ground. I was devastated. I felt humiliated. I also felt as though I never wanted to give out another tract. Ever!

Rejection is a powerful blow to human pride. It cuts deep, like a burning arrow in the heart. It makes the most courageous of us want to withdraw in defeat. It is when that sharp arrow pierces the flesh that we need to think of the sinful woman of whom the Bible speaks in Luke 7:36–50.

She came into the house of a Pharisee, stood behind Jesus, and began to wash His feet with her tears. Perhaps she quietly approached the Master as He lay at a table in typical Middle-Eastern fashion— on His side with His feet stretched out behind Him. As she listened to His gracious words, tears of contrition began to fall in great droplets onto His feet. We are told that (for some reason) the Pharisee didn't follow the custom of the day and wash the feet of his guests as they entered his home. As her tears mingled with the dust that was on Jesus' feet, she dropped to her knees and began to dry His feet with her hair. A woman's hair is her glory, but she so humbled herself that she forgot her natural vanity, and dried His dusty and wet feet with the locks of her hair.

Those who have heard the Savior's gracious words and seen their own sinful condition fall at the feet of Jesus and wash them in tears of contrition. They can be clothed with humility because they have been stripped of their pride and of this life's vanities. At the feet of the Savior, they understand that all that really matters is the approval of God. It is there that His will becomes their will. They too will want to have beautiful feet, shod with the preparation of the gospel of peace.

Then, when the world casts stones of rejection,

we will look to the heavens and see Jesus standing at the right hand of God. When they nail our hands and feet to a cross of restraint, we still seek only the approval of God. When they offer the vinegar of bitter scorn so that fear causes our tongues to stick to our jaws, we will still speak, because we seek only the smile of God.

The next time you gaze at the moon, realize that its light is actually the result of solar radiation from a star so big that the earth fits into its volume a million times. This light was sent 93 million miles in a straight line traveling at 186,000 miles per second and hit dirt on the face of the moon. The light then was reflected toward the earth and traveled another 250,000 miles at the same speed, so that you could have soft light in the darkness of the night.

> We are surrounded by many such miracles, but we don't give them a second thought.

We are surrounded by many such miracles, but we don't give them a second thought. If we did, we would begin to comprehend that God is the Maker of this incredible creation that we so take for granted. When we see the unspeakable greatness of His power, we will recognize the importance of seeking His approval rather than that of the lowly dust He shaped into man by His miracle-working hand.

The moonlight will also remind us of the fact that even though we are called "children of light," we don't have our own light. We merely reflect the light of Jesus, the Light of the World. One day He will reveal Himself in flaming fire. The pain of our rejection by this world pales compared to the unspeakable terror of the world's rejection by God.

The first time Jesus preached in his hometown His hearers were so wrath-filled that they tried to kill Him by throwing Him off a cliff (see Luke 4:29). But He didn't end His ministry simply because He was despised and rejected by men. Instead, He "committed Himself to Him who judges righteously." He looked to the smile of a holy God, rather than the frown of a sinful world.

So the next time you let your little light shine by preaching the gospel or giving out a tract, and a bucking bronco throws you for a loop, chews you up, and spits you onto the soil, remember the moonlight. Remember how it just reflects the brilliance of the sun. Then get up and find another horse, and get back into the saddle...while there is still time.

CHAPTER TEN

The Power of Humor

Have you ever driven a car toward the rising sun? Its glare is painful. It hinders you from seeing anything clearly. However, if you turn around and drive in the direction that the sun's rays are shining, everything you view will become clear. That's what happens at conversion. When a man's heart drives against the Law, the things of God frustrate and anger him. The Law's powerful rays spoil his outlook on sin. But the moment he turns from sin and places his faith in Jesus, he sees all things clearly. He knows the truth and the truth makes him free.

Have you ever seen the Law do its work? If not, then experiment with it. The next time you speak to an atheist who says, "I don't believe in God," just say, "Okay. Do you consider yourself to be a good person?" Learn the art of circumnavigating the intellect. When he says that he does, ask, "Have you ever told a lie?" If he has, ask, "What does that make you?" Have him confess that he is a "liar." Ask if he has ever stolen something. If he says no, say (in a friendly tone), "Come on…you've just admitted to me that you're a liar. Have you ever stolen anything in your whole life, even if it's small?" If he says yes, ask what that makes him—"a thief." Then say, "Jesus said, 'Whoever looks at a woman to lust for her has already committed adultery with her in his heart.' Have you ever looked with lust?" If he has, gently say, "What's your name?" ("John.") "John, by your own admission, you are a lying, thieving, adulterer at heart, and we've only looked at three of the Ten Commandments."

Take the same approach with a Mormon, a Muslim, an intellectual—anyone to whom you want to witness. Most Christians think that they have to bury their heads in the Koran or the Book of Mormon before they can witness effectively to those groups. Not so. Just bury your head in the Bible. God's Word is sufficient. When you lift up your head you should have your brain filled with these truths: "By the Law is the knowledge of sin" (Romans 3:20); "I would not have known sin except through the Law" (Romans 7:7); "The Law was a schoolmaster to bring us to Christ" (Galatians 3:24); and "The Law is good if anyone uses it lawfully" (1 Timothy 1:8).

After studying Scripture you should know that the area of battle isn't the sinner's intellect, it's his conscience. So if you just want to argue, stay in the intellect; but if you want to see sinners surrender to Jesus Christ, move the battle into the conscience, using the Law of God to bring the knowledge of sin.

Don't be afraid to use humor to soften a stranger's heart. If you think that you don't have the "gift of humor," we can help you. Go to our web site at www.raycomfort.com and click on "The Power of Humor."

I often use humor when I want to speak with a stranger. As I was flying from Phoenix to California, I was seated next to a young couple. I introduced myself and continued to type on my laptop. As I typed, I noticed out of the corner of my eye that the young lady pulled out a large plastic bottle of water and took a drink. Her husband then held out his hand for the bottle and took a drink. Without looking up, I reached out my hand to take the bottle for *my* drink. That made them both laugh. We talked a little (and laughed some more), and so I felt at liberty to take a risk. As the plane took off I pressed the button on the man's armrest, causing his seat to go back as we lifted into the air. That sent his wife into hysterics. From then on, both of them were very friendly. I told them about my connection to Kirk, which gave me an entrance into the things of God. I asked, "Are you Christians?" They both told me that they were, but the husband said that he had not been born again. I asked if they thought they were good people. Both did, but he turned out to be a lying, thieving, adulterer at heart. She was a liar, a thief, and a blasphemer. As I talked about the cross, tears welled in their eyes. She said it was amazing that I was speaking to them, because she had just told her husband that they should start going to church. I didn't press for a "decision" from them, but instead encouraged them to seek the Lord in repentance and establish a prayer life together.

The next day the husband returned an e-mail from me saying that they really appreciated the chat we had. If you see "success" in witnessing as simply faithfully planting the seed of God's Word in the hearts of sinners, then you will find much success. If you think that you have to get "decisions" from sinners, you will often be discouraged.

The Bible says that our ministry is to sow seed. If we sow, someone somewhere will reap. He who sows and he who reaps will rejoice together. He who sows is nothing and he who reaps is nothing, but the glory belongs to God, who causes the seed to grow. Once we understand that, and let God do His work, then we will see sinners come to Christ and "bring forth fruit."

About fifty feet from my office window was a man selling hot dogs. I would pass Mike every day as I went to the courthouse to hand out tracts. One day he stopped me and began to talk. I took the opportunity to go through the Law with him, and then encouraged him to cross the road and take a tour of our ministry some time.

When he came by that afternoon, I showed him around, and as he was leaving he asked if we could talk further about the things of God. We made an appointment for 7:00 the next morning.

When Mike arrived, he made it clear that he wanted to give his life to Jesus Christ. I had him pray, then I prayed for him and gave him some literature. As he was leaving, he stopped at my office door and said, "You have no idea what this has meant to me." He come over later that morning and gave hot dogs to our staff. The question then arose, "Are hot dogs 'fruit'?" We came to the conclusion that they were, and time proved us right.

Typical Comfort

I had been the guest speaker at the graduation of ten students at a Christian school in Reno, Nevada. As the congregation of about 200 people joined in prayer for each individual student, I surmised that I could sneak off the stage and call Kirk to see how he was doing. So that's what I did. I snuck down the aisle while every eye was closed and every head bowed.

Kirk didn't answer his phone, so I left a message that we would be eating out that night at a casino. (Casinos offer cheap food, gambling that if you go there to eat, you will also gamble. They lose because we eat and leave.) I then snuck back up onto the stage while the next student was being prayed for. The mission was successful—no one had even noticed that I had left. Suddenly my phone rang. I hadn't switched off the ringer, and as I had only had the phone for 18 months, I wasn't familiar with how to do that quickly, so I stuffed the phone in my armpit and ran down the aisle. That's when I realized how many people pray with their eyes open. I could hear controlled laughter throughout the congregation.

As I neared the back of the sanctuary, I heard the sound of my glasses falling out of my shirt pocket. I dropped to my knees in the semidarkness, opened the phone and heard, "Hello, Ray." I whispered, "Kirk! I can't talk right now...hang on a moment." Then I spent the next minute or so vainly searching for my glasses, which must have slid beneath the pews (I couldn't see where they had gone because I didn't have my glasses on). I had to enlist help in finding them, and when the prayer time ended, I asked everyone in the vicinity not to move their feet in case they stepped on my glasses. Fortunately, someone found them and handed them to me. I then went back to my conversation with Kirk, who laughed as he said, "Hey...first I hear that you are off to a casino, then all I hear is whispering. What's going on?"

The above incident isn't isolated. I am a walking disaster. If you don't believe it, ask Mark Spence. He often shakes his head in disbelief when he learns what happens to me. If I have a hammer in my hand, my wife gets a Band-Aid (see my book *Comfort, the Feebleminded*). If I build anything, it is bound to collapse (ask my daughter). One day, Jacob (my eldest son) and I went home to load my van with boxes of books from our garage. I backed the vehicle up to the garage door, careful not to knock over any of Sue's potted plants. As we were loading, I noticed that I had come close to the plants, but thankfully hadn't knocked any over.

When we arrived at the ministry and went around to the back of the van to unload, much to our surprise we found that one of Sue's plants was hanging out of the back door of the vehicle. I had slammed the door and taken some extra baggage along—one of Sue's potted plants. Everyone is amazed at how I manage to do things like that so often.

That night Sue and I arrived home and couldn't get up our driveway. It was blocked by a large plant holder. I had managed to drag it the full length of our driveway before ripping out one plant and driving away. Sue wasn't surprised.

Shortly after that, I was asked by a friend to call a key pastor named Bob in a large church. The reason for the call was to make contact for future ministry. The conversation went well. Very well.

> I am a walking disaster. If I have a hammer in my hand, my wife gets a Band-Aid.

We laughed, spoke of the things of God, and even talked about our common interest in surfing. He said that he would get back to me, and he sounded very sincere. As the conversation wound down I felt humbly proud of myself. I had left a good impression. However, after he said good-bye, I heard myself conclude, "Bob bless you, God. Bye."

My Cup Runneth Over

It was 4:30 in the morning. Kirk and I were in South Carolina. The pastor was picking us up at 4:55 a.m. to take us to the airport and Kirk wasn't answering his cell phone. He had apparently slept in! He was fortunate to have me traveling with him. I had done this hundreds of times. Kirk was a comparative novice.

Despite the fact that I was only half dressed, I went across the hall and knocked on his door. I knocked once. Twice. No answer! Suddenly I heard a familiar *click!* My door had shut, leaving me in the hallway, half dressed. No matter. The important thing was to wake up Kirk. I ran down the hallway to the front desk so they could call him.

As I entered the reception area, there was Kirk—fully dressed, casually drinking a cup of coffee, and witnessing to an officer of the law! Meanwhile, I was half asleep, half dressed, and locked out of my room, and I had three people staring at me as though I was some sort of nut.

A few hours later we were on a plane heading for Los Angeles, with a woman named Hope sitting next to us. Kirk accidentally knocked over his cup of hot coffee onto his lap. What was his reaction as that boiling liquid hit his tender flesh? Did he go, "Man, that hurt!"? Yes, he did. He felt the pain. (I think I've heard that somewhere before.) Actually, he *yelled* with pain. It was a blessing that I was there to help. I quickly grabbed napkins and handed them to him. That's what friends are for. Suddenly, I knocked over my ice water onto my lap. Man, it was cold!

All sign of Hope had gone as soon as Kirk had spilled his coffee. Fortunately she reappeared with a stack of napkins. Hope does not disappoint. We both had wet right legs—his was hot and mine was cold. It reminded us that Jesus said we should be either hot or cold as Christians.

The next time the flight attendant came by to offer us drinks, Hope asked her for a couple of kids' "sippy" cups.

I have mentioned these incidents for a reason. After reading about some of the events in this book, you may get the impression that I'm something I'm not—and if you put anyone up on a pedestal you may find it hard to reach the things they are reaching. *Any* Christian can do the things that I have done, because it is *God* who is at work in each of us. It is a level playing field. The great key to being used by God is to realize that He uses "nobodys" from nowhere, who have nothing to offer Him but a surrendered heart.

Recently a young man called to tell me how he was on fire for God. I was surprised because the last time I spoke to him he was a professing Christian, but was deeply depressed and suicidal. When I asked what caused him to turn his life around, he simply said, "Total surrender." He explained that the root of his depression and suicidal thoughts was selfishness. That really is the key. Total surrender. No more selfishness. Slam the door on sin and self, and don't drag along any extra baggage.

Part of total surrender is to know that when the world says you have "rights," you know that you don't have any. They were given up at Calvary. When the world says something that seems to make sense, you filter it through the Word of God, and if it's not in line with Scripture, you throw it out. God's ways are not the ways of the world. Take for instance how I have learned to respond to angry e-mails (we sell millions of tracts each year, and each one lists our web site address). A man named Tony wrote to me and stated, "Hey, thanks for the handout I received at a concert last night." He then said that he had used it in the bathroom, and ended his letter with "Satan loves you!"

I wrote back a simple, "Thanks, Tony. I appreciate you letting us know. God bless, Ray." His response was interesting: "I like your style. You at least follow the teachings of Jesus in your human interactions. I take back the Satan stuff. Peace to you. Tony."

I wrote again to tell him about myself, the area where I lived, etc. When he responded by telling me that he was a professing atheist, I asked if he would like a free copy of *God Doesn't Believe in Atheists*. He did, and he sent me his address.

Another e-mail read:

> Hi Ray,
> I was not very pleased to read the !*$&@ about God and Jesus. First of all: Jesus is dead.

For almost 2000 years. Why should you pray to a dead man? Second: God is !*$%@. Have you ever seen him? Stupid Americans. Killing each other all day with your guns, people are starving and still believe in that !*$%@. Stop it now, it's a waste of time. Don't ever send me again something about god or j-sus, I hate them. And I hate Muslims too of course. Thijs from Holland

I replied:

Thijs. Thanks for taking the time to share your thoughts. Holland is a beautiful land. I was in Amsterdam a couple of years ago. Loved it. Again, thanks for writing. Ray

He quickly responded with:

Hi Ray,
Thank you too for your nice answer. Happy to hear you like Holland! See you, and sorry for my first e-mail. Thijs Scheijvens

We have access to the most powerful of weapons—love. So the next time someone abuses you for your faith, don't react the way you feel like reacting. Instead, think what love would do. Then do it.

I noticed that a rather macho friend of mine lacked verbal expression of love for his wife, so I decided that I would help him. When she called him on his cell phone, he answered with a typical unromantic, "What's up?" I looked at him earnestly and whispered, "I love you...I love you," and gestured to let his wife know that fact. He glanced at me and said, "Ray says he loves you," and without missing a beat, carried on with his conversation.

My friend did love his wife, but love without *any* expression at all is an oxymoron. It is food with no taste, fire without heat, music without sound. So don't let love be passive. Openly show your love for God and man by making a diligent search for hearts open to the gospel.

As a nation we have forsaken God's Law, and America is reaping the sad consequences. If we were able to completely fulfill the Law, we wouldn't need civil law. But the more Lawlessness abounds, the more we need civil laws. If a nation fulfills the Law (in Christ), it reaps national harmony instead of the chaos we now see.

> Owe no one anything except to love one another, for he who loves another has fulfilled the law. For the commandments, "You shall not commit adultery," "You shall not murder," "You shall not steal," "You shall not bear false witness," "You shall not covet," and if there is any other commandment, are all summed up in this saying, namely, "You shall love your neighbor as yourself." Love does no harm to a neighbor; therefore love is the fulfillment of the law (Romans 13:8–10).

In other words, if we love someone we won't covet his goods or his wife. Nor will we lie to him, steal from him, commit adultery with his wife, kill him, or even hate him. That means there would be no theft, no rape, no murder, no prejudice, no violence, no robbery, no greed, no adultery, no lawsuits, etc. How society would change!

In August 2002, I was summoned for jury duty. Four years earlier a man had been following a truck on the freeway when a number of cardboard boxes flew off the truck, causing this man to swerve, apparently injuring his neck and back. The driver of the truck had since died. Presumably the injured man had no insurance, so he was in court suing the trucking company.

Suddenly it was prime-time courtroom drama. There was a gasp in the gallery.

The jury selection was slow and boring. One at a time, the prospective jurors would be subjected to the same tedious questions. The judge would begin with, "How are you?" After the person answered, he would ask, "Do you think you can be impartial in this case?" There would be a predictable, "Yes," and then further predictable, tedious questions.

After a number of people had been questioned and many dismissed, my name was called. As I sat in the jury box, the judge turned to me and asked the expected, "How are you?" I told him that I was fine.

Then he asked, "Do you think you can be impartial in this case?" I looked at him and answered, "No." Suddenly it was prime-time courtroom drama. There was a gasp in the gallery. He looked startled and said, "Wha...!" Tension filled the air. He asked, "What do you mean?" When I requested a "sidebar," he suggested that I talk to his bailiff.

I walked across to the bailiff and said, "I am honored to be an American citizen, but I find the American custom of suing each other to be abhorrent—especially in this case when there has been an obvious accident." I then told him that I was a pastor and that I believe we should love our neighbor as much as we love ourselves, and that meant we didn't sue him. I concluded with, "I wouldn't give this guy a bean."

The bailiff smiled and said, "I will do my best to relate this to the judge." The lawyers, the judge, and the bailiff then gathered in a huddle. As the judge glanced over at me I heard him say, "Cultural..." Then he looked at me and said, "Good-bye."

I would have liked to have added that the only thing all this suing is doing is lining the pockets of greedy lawyers, but I thought I had better quit while I was ahead.

CHAPTER ELEVEN

Dr. Luke's Cure

America is deathly sick. Lawsuits are only a tiny part of the problem. The nightly network news has become a parade for competing drug companies. Both in news content and advertising, we are informed of new drugs that will help in the fight against an onslaught of illnesses from prostate cancer to heart disease. The problem is that most of these breakthroughs tend to have side effects that sound almost as bad as the disease.

Added to this are news items telling us of invading killer bees, killer mosquitoes, killer tornadoes, child killers, kids who kill kids, kids who kill parents, unprecedented droughts, out-of-control fires, horrific murder-suicides, corporate fraud, massive layoffs, falling stocks, and much, much more, and it is no exaggeration to say that America is sick, from sea to shining sea.

Those who know their Bibles suspect that there's more here than meets the eye. They have studied the promised repercussions for the nation of Israel if they didn't abide by certain God-given principles. They then look at the United States and see striking parallels between America and what happened to Israel. For example, Deuteronomy 28 tells us that if the Israelites forsook the Ten Commandments (see Deuteronomy 27), certain terrible things would happen. They would be struck with diseases in their children and in their land. They would be plagued with mildew (mold), terrible drought, horrific and incurable diseases, irrational fears, marriage breakdown, repossession, and bankruptcy. Their children would be taken from them, their crops would be diseased, and aliens would invade their borders.

These were parallels I noticed right through the 1990s. Almost everything lined up—everything, that is, except an invasion by enemies. Deuteronomy warned of that, but that threat appeared to be one that was peculiar to the nation of Israel. It couldn't apply to this country. America was the one and only superpower of the world. No weapon that was formed against us could prosper. Great oceans protected us from any enemy attack—that is, up until September 11, 2001.

Sadly, when the enemy struck our nation, few said that the incident had anything to do with God. We had forsaken the Ten Commandments, sanctioned millions of abortions, loved violence, adultery, pornography, etc., but it was unthinkable that America's sins called for God's chastening hand.

Unfortunately, the conscience of our nation failed to do its duty. In recent years the Church as a whole has been deathly silent when it comes to having a clear evangelistic voice. According to Bill Bright, the founder of Campus Crusade for Christ, only 2 percent of Christians actively share their faith. That means (for some reason) 98 percent don't. But more than that, even many of the 2 percent who share their faith fail to use the Ten Commandments within their sphere of influence. This was the way Jesus presented the gospel (Luke 18:18–22), but most don't follow His example. They instead follow the traditions of modern evangelism, and therefore strip the gospel of its power. If we discard the bow, we shouldn't wonder why the arrow has no thrust.

Consequently the Church's light has been snuffed out in the darkness of the hour in which we live. Its savor has been lost. It has become good for nothing but to be trampled underfoot by men.

The Gospel of Luke diagnoses the nation's disease and thankfully gives us the certain cure. Luke 10:2 tells us what it is. There is a lack of laborers—laborers who have been raised up by God.

We have been obeying the admonition to pray for laborers, and *you* are the answer to our prayers. You are the needed salt and light. We would be bold enough to say that one big step in the right direction is for you to get "The Way of the Master" video series. It has been designed to train you for the job of sharing the gospel. View it for yourself and see how God is using it to equip and enthuse the most lukewarm of Christians. You may even be stirred enough to hold a seminar and screen the series to those who have the unction to show up.

Then again, if we want to reach the lost, we should ask ourselves how much we want true revival. Would our churches be radical enough to change the order of our Sunday morning service and show the series to the church? Perhaps that's asking too much. The order of service is a tradition. To change it and equip the saints is a little too radical—and that may bring about what we profess to be praying for: genuine God-ordained revival.

The Master

Kirk had received a master of *Left Behind II: Tribulation Force*, but hadn't viewed it because he didn't like to watch himself act. We were both concerned that the editors might for some reason decide to remove the Ten Commandments from the gospel scene, so I couldn't wait until my copy arrived to see if they had left it in.

A few days later I had it in my hands. I was apprehensive as I pushed "Play" on the remote. The movie started off a little slow, but it wasn't long until I was pulled into the story. The gospel scene was just as it was shot—nothing changed, nothing removed! But more than that, I had forgotten that we had also suggested rewrites for the scene with the two witnesses at the Wailing Wall. Instead of simply preaching grace, we had them quote Old Testament verses about God's omniscience and the fact that He will bring every work to judgment, including every secret thing. Then we had the Rabbi say that he had kept the Commandments from his youth, followed by one of the witnesses telling him that no one will be made right with God by keeping the Law—that we are saved by grace and grace alone (God's unmerited favor). Then came the good news of the cross. I was ecstatic. I shouted for joy and wept at the same time.

A few minutes after the movie ended, Kirk happened to call. I raved big time! He then watched it, and wrote the following in our monthly e-mail newsletter:[8]

"I couldn't bring myself to watch it for a week. I finally watched it and was thrilled!"

> I was initially given a rough cut of the movie, which has 80% of the film cut and scored with temporary music and sound effects. I didn't watch it, and decided to wait for the final version. When Ray and I were sent the final copy from Cloud Ten, he watched it immediately, then told me how much he loved it. Honestly, I was nervous about the final outcome. I so wanted it to be good that I couldn't bring myself to watch it for a week. I finally watched it and was thrilled! Although I'm incredibly critical of any project I work on, I have

to say that I believe this movie is better than *Left Behind* Part 1 and certainly has tremendous evangelistic potential. I think you're going to love it.

One thought that comes to mind as I watch the movie is how good some of the acting is. Brad Johnson (who plays Rayford Steele) does an incredible job in the movie witnessing to his pilot buddy Chris. After listening to the evangelistic words coming out of his mouth, it's hard to believe that Brad is not a Christian. I had the chance to witness to him personally for about an hour as we rehearsed our lines, Ray shared with him for several minutes on different occasions on the set, and Brad's wife is born again. God is incredible—using a non-Christian actor to effectively communicate the gospel of everlasting life to non-Christians like himself. Perhaps when Brad watches the movie, "Rayford" will convince Brad and he'll be saved!

A week or so later, reviews of the movie started pouring in:

> Dr. Jack Van Impe: "I've never seen a Christian film that's its equal. The soul-winning potential of this film is staggering. Millions could be touched by its message."

> Dr. Ted Baehr, Founder, Christian Film and Television Commission: "The evangelistic power of this film is awesome! Characters repeat-

edly come to Christ in powerfully acted and compelling scenes."

Randall Murphree, Editor, *American Family Association Journal*: "On a scale of one to ten, it's a ten."

Tom Saab, Founder and Director, Christian Film Festivals of America, Inc.: "Finally, a superb 'end-times' thriller that can truly be used for evangelism and is guaranteed to lead thousands to a saving knowledge of Jesus Christ. Throughout the film individuals receive Jesus as Lord and Savior in ways that will touch the most stubborn and cynical heart... In addition, the producers, writers, and directors made sure that sin, repentance, and forgiveness were mentioned and they emphasized that acknowledging our sin, turning away from it, and asking God's forgiveness were an essential part of receiving Jesus as Savior and Lord. There are not just a few powerful and moving scenes in this film as most Christian films have, but numerous sequences throughout every part of the movie that will have you crying or cheering, tug at your heart, cause you to think, and definitely inspire you to go out and share the gospel of Jesus Christ with a lost and dying world.

On the morning I locked myself out of my hotel room and found Kirk sharing the gospel with a policeman, the officer walked out of the doors of the hotel and hollered back, "I'll see you in the movies." Kirk smiled and said, "Yes, but I want to see *you* in heaven." That's the bottom line. Make sure you are there, and once you have trusted in the Savior, take the light to others who are still sitting in the shadow of death.

When we were revising the Ten Commandments scene, we had no idea that it was a miracle in the making. But God is like that. He tends to quietly work in our lives.

Perhaps He's working a miracle in your life right now.

Notes

1. Listen to Kirk Cameron share this teaching on www.WayOfTheMaster.com.

2. For the full encounter, see *How to Win Souls and Influence People* (Bridge-Logos Publishers).

3. To grow further in your faith, read your Bible every day and obey what you read. For practical steps of spiritual growth, visit our web site at: www.WayOfTheMaster.com and click on "Spiritual Bread."

4. Published by Bridge-Logos Publishers.

5. The video, *BC-AD: Barrier-Comfort Atheism Debate*, is available through Living Waters Publications, 800-437-1893 or www.raycomfort.com.

6. See www.raycomfort.com.

7. A few weeks later we received an e-mail from a woman who had heard about this incident. She said that she went for a walk and specifically asked God if she should add Kirk and me to her prayer list. As she prayed, a butterfly hit her in the head. Then another one did the same thing.

8. Freely available at www.WayOfTheMaster.com.

Way of the Master Academy

I f you would like to learn how to effectively share your faith, check out our school of biblical evangelism called "The Way of the Master Academy" at www.WayOfTheMaster.com.

Here are some commendations from students:

"The School is absolutely awesome; I have been truly blessed by this ministry." **Pastor Brent Wisdom** (CA)

"I cannot explain how blessed I get every time I open the School of Evangelism and study. I have pastored for almost eleven years and have never been to Bible School. Until now! Thank you so much for this great work." **Pastor Wayne Andres** (MD)

"SOBE is opening a completely new world of understanding regarding the gospel and God working in peoples lives." **Rick Todd** (SC)

"I am 42 and have shared my belief in Christ for almost 20 years but I have never seen anything as powerful as the teaching I have received from the School of Biblical Evangelism." **James W. Smith** (TX)

"As a graduate of EE and every other evangelism course I can find, yours by far has been the best." **Bill Lawson** (NY)